D1105410

# ZULU

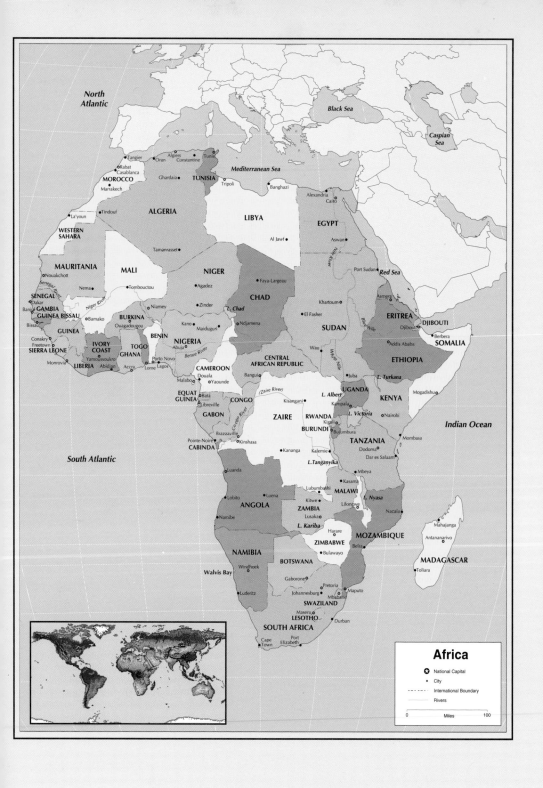

**North Atlantic**

Black Sea

Caspian Sea

Tangier
Oran Algiers Constantine Tunis
Rabat
Casablanca
**MOROCCO** Ghardaia **TUNISIA** Tripoli
Marrakech Banghazi
Mediterranean Sea
Alexandria
La'youn Tindouf Cairo
**WESTERN SAHARA** **ALGERIA** **LIBYA** **EGYPT**
Tamanrasset Al Jawf
Aswan
**MAURITANIA** Port Sudan **Red Sea**
Nouakchott **MALI** **NIGER** Faya-Largeau
Nema Agadez Asmera
Tombouctou **CHAD** Khartoum **ERITREA**
Niger River Niamey Zinder Ndjamena Djibouti **DJIBOUTI**
**SENEGAL** Bamako Kano L. Chad El Fasher **SUDAN** Addis Ababa Berbera
Dakar
**GAMBIA** **BURKINA** Maiduguri Wau **SOMALIA**
Banjul Ouagadougou White Nile Juba **ETHIOPIA**
Bissau **GUINEA BISSAU** **BENIN** **NIGERIA** Benue River **CENTRAL** **AFRICAN REPUBLIC** L. Turkana
**GUINEA** Abuja
Conakry **IVORY** **TOGO** Mogadishu
Freetown **COAST** **GHANA** Porto Novo Bangui **CAMEROON** L. Albert **UGANDA** **KENYA**
**SIERRA LEONE** Yamoussoukro Lome Douala Kisangani Kampala
Monrovia **LIBERIA** Abidjan Accra Lagos Malabo **(Zaire River)** L. Victoria Nairobi
Yaounde **Indian Ocean**
**EQUAT.** Bata **CONGO** **ZAIRE** **RWANDA** Kigali
**GUINEA** Libreville **BURUNDI** Bujumbura Mombasa
**GABON** Brazzaville **TANZANIA** Dodoma
**South Atlantic** Pointe-Noire Kinshasa Kananga Kalemie Dar es Salaam
**CABINDA** L. Tanganyika Mbeya
Luanda Kasama
Lubumbashi **MALAWI** L. Nyasa
Lobito Luena Kitwe Lilongwe Nacala
**ANGOLA** **ZAMBIA** Lusaka
Namibe L. Kariba Harare Mahajanga
Antananarivo
**ZIMBABWE** Belra **MOZAMBIQUE**
Bulawayo **MADAGASCAR**
**NAMIBIA** **BOTSWANA** Toliara
Windhoek
Walvis Bay Gaborone Pretoria
Luderitz Johannesburg Mbabane Maputo
**SWAZILAND**
Maseru Durban
**LESOTHO**
**SOUTH AFRICA**
Cape Town Port Elizabeth

**Africa**

⊛ National Capital
• City
‑‑‑ International Boundary
— Rivers

0 Miles 100

The Heritage Library of African Peoples

# ZULU

Zolani Ngwane

THE ROSEN PUBLISHING GROUP, INC.
NEW YORK

Published in 1997 by The Rosen Publishing Group, Inc.
29 East 21st Street, New York, NY 10010

Copyright 1997 by The Rosen Publishing Group, Inc.

First Edition

Manufactured in the United States of America

**Library of Congress Cataloging-in-Publication Data**


Ngwane, Zolani.
    Zulu / Zolani Ngwane. — 1st ed.
        p.   cm. — (The heritage library of African peoples)
    Includes bibliographical references and index.
    Summary: Surveys the culture, history, and contemporary life of the Zulu people of South Africa.
    ISBN 0-8239-2014-3
    1. Zulu (African people)—History—Juvenile literature.   2. Zulu (African people)—Social life and customs—Juvenile literature.
I. Title.  II. Series.
DT1768.Z95N39   1996
968'.004963986—dc20                                96-42293
                                                   CIP
                                                   AC

# Contents

# INTRODUCTION

**THERE IS EVERY REASON FOR US TO KNOW** something about Africa and to understand its past and the way of life of its peoples. Africa is a rich continent that has for centuries provided the world with art, culture, labor, wealth, and natural resources. It has vast mineral deposits, fossil fuels, and commercial crops.

But perhaps most important is the fact that fossil evidence indicates that human beings originated in Africa. The earliest traces of human beings and their tools are almost two million years old. Their descendants have migrated throughout the world. To be human is to be of African descent.

The experiences of the peoples who stayed in Africa are as rich and as diverse as of those who established themselves elsewhere. This series of books describes their environment, their modes of subsistence, their relationships, and their customs and beliefs. The books present the variety of languages, histories, cultures, and religions that are to be found on the African continent. They demonstrate the historical linkages between African peoples and the way contemporary Africa has been affected by European colonial rule.

Africa is large, complex, and diverse. It encompasses an area of more than 11,700,000 square miles. The United States, Europe, and India could fit easily into it. The sheer size is an indication of the continent's great variety in geography, terrain, climate, flora, fauna, peoples, languages, and cultures.

Much of contemporary Africa has been shaped by European colonial rule, industrialization, urbanization, and the demands of a world economic system. For more than seventy years, large regions of Africa were ruled by Great Britain, France, Belgium, Portugal, and Spain. African peoples from various ethnic, linguistic, and cultural backgrounds were brought together to form colonial states.

For decades Africans struggled to gain their independence. It was not until after World War II that the colonial territories became independent African states. Today, almost all of Africa is ruled by Africans. Large numbers of Africans live in modern cities. Rural Africa is also being transformed, and yet its people still engage in many of their customs and beliefs.

Contemporary circumstances and natural events have not always been kind to ordinary Africans. Today, however, new popular social movements and technological innovations pose great promise for future development.

George C. Bond, Ph.D., Director
Institute of African Studies
Columbia University, New York

The Zulu people have played a major role in the history of southern Africa. Many Zulu today are keen supporters of Zulu tradition. The woman above wears a cape decorated with beadwork, a traditional art form made by women.

# chapter

# 1

# THE LAND AND THE PEOPLE

**IN THE ZULU LANGUAGE,** *AMAZULU* **MEANS** the Zulu people, and the word *zulu* means heaven. According to a Zulu version of the creation story, this name refers to the belief that the Zulu people came down from heaven.

## ▼ ZULU HISTORY ▼

The Zulu people have played a major role in the history of southern Africa for the last two hundred years. They rose to power under their great chief Shaka (1787–1828). A military genius, he built the small Zulu chiefdom into a powerful kingdom that controlled much of the eastern coast of South Africa in the early 1800s.

Shaka brought under his control many other weaker chiefdoms in the region. These various groups had similar traditions, languages, and customs to the Zulu. They had no choice but to

## CREATION

The Zulu name for the Supreme Being and Creator is Mvelingqangi (pronounced m-vell-een-KUNG-gi), which means He who came first. The Zulu god lives in heaven. Mvelingqangi lowered his two children, a man and a woman, down from heaven attached to an umbilical cord. On earth, they cut themselves free with a sharp reed. This is how the Zulu came to be named after heaven. This is also why members of the Zulu royal family are referred to as *abantwana*, or children, because they are all descended from Mvelingqangi's children.

Another popular creation story states that people emerged from deep in the earth through a moist bed of reeds. As in other southern African creation stories reeds play a key role.

Today, however, largely because of the influence of Christianity, most Zulu would suggest that all people, not only the Zulu, were created by Mvelingqangi, who then scattered them all over the world. Some substitute Mvelingqangi with the Christian God.

become part of the Zulu Kingdom. Together with the Zulu, all the peoples in this region are known as the North Nguni people.

It is not known exactly when the Zulu settled where they are now or formed a separate chiefdom. However, European sailors' records show that the Zululand coast was inhabited by the mid-1500s. Until the time of Shaka, the Zulu chiefdom was small.

## ZULU CRAFTS

The Zulu are famous for their fine crafts.

Zulu pottery includes containers of many different shapes. Still made today, these pots are shaped by hand from wet clay, decorated with engraved designs, and then baked in homemade ovens.

Zulu gourds are popular with collectors today. They were used to hold finely ground tobacco called snuff, or other substances. Many are decorated with metal wire, beads, or designs engraved into the surface. The beer gourd called *ukhamba* is still widely used.

Zulu women continue to use wild grasses to weave baskets, food containers, and mats. The grass is often colored with natural dyes and woven into beautiful designs.

Many of these traditional, hand-crafted arts are now mass-produced in factories and sold all over the world.

Seen above are different stages of pottery making. After the clay is kneaded, the pot is formed and decorated. The boys on the right are smoothing the surfaces of the pots.

Because of their major confrontations with white forces during the 1800s, the Zulu people became world famous. These battles have been dramatized in movies such as "Zulu" and the television series "Shaka Zulu," which have been seen around the world. The Zulu fought several wars against the British. They also resisted the Dutch settlers known as Boers or Afrikaners. Though often victorious against the whites, the Zulu Kingdom was eventually defeated.

## ▼ THE ZULU IN THE 1900S ▼

During the 1900s, the Zulu, like all black groups in South Africa, suffered under oppressive white rule. They had no right to vote and few freedoms. Most importantly, under the South African system of segregation called apartheid, black peoples were forced to live in "homelands" or reservations.

Homeland borders often included some land that black groups had lived on before the whites came. However, the best land was taken away by whites. The name homelands was misleading because the land given to the blacks often did not include peoples' original home areas. Under apartheid, black people had to have permits to leave these poor homelands and find work in white areas. The Zulu homeland was known as Kwazulu.

The politics of the South African homeland

## BEADWORK

Beads were a major item of early trade with Europeans. During much of the twentieth century, southern Africa was one of the world's major destinations for glass beads. Its peoples produced fine art works from beads. All beaded pieces both reflected individual creativity and followed regional patterns and colors. Combined with other aspects of costume such as women's hairdos, beadwork expresses a great deal about people—including where they come from, their marital status, and other groups to which they may belong. The beadwork of diviners and members of the Shembe Church is among the most impressive examples of Zulu art. Beadwork is also popular with tourists.

Fantastic beaded outfits are worn by Zulu rickshaw men (above). The rickshaw, introduced to South Africa from Asia, is a small buggy pulled by a strong person. Rickshaw rides are popular with tourists.

## IZANGOMA (DIVINERS)

Diviners have special spiritual powers. *Izangoma* (singular: *sangoma*) diagnose physical, psychological, and spiritual problems by "throwing the bones." The *sangoma* throws a collection of small animal bones and other significant and symbolic objects onto the ground. Together with the help of the spirits of the ancestors, the diviner diagnoses problems and prescribes remedies by "reading" the lay of the bones on the ground.

Diviners often prescribe an animal sacrifice to honor the ancestors. Some remedies also include brewing traditional beer, a beverage made from grain and containing little alcohol. Some beer is spilled onto the ground for the ancestors before the people drink it.

Sometimes persistent sickness is interpreted as a sign that the spirits of the ancestors are calling a person to become a *sangoma*.

The Zulu also recognize other specialists. An *inyanga*, or healer, uses herbs to heal bodily ailments. An *inyanga yezulu* is a rainmaker. This person has the extraordinary power to plead with the ancestors to send the rain that is necessary for the continuation of life.

system were complex. Many homeland leaders were viewed as puppets who cooperated with the white government of South Africa. They often acted against the wishes of their own people whom they were supposed to represent. Other black leaders tried to use the homeland system to win benefits for their people. However, the majority of South Africans rejected apartheid and the homeland system that was its cornerstone.

Zulu diviners usually wear beaded headdresses and very impressive outfits. This diviner's
at includes inflated goat bladders and chicken feathers. These animals have been sacrificed to
he ancestors in religious ceremonies. Therefore this hat is a sign of spiritual activity and power.

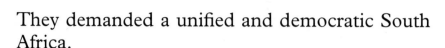

They demanded a unified and democratic South Africa.

After many years of struggle and violence, these goals were achieved in 1994 when South Africa held its first democratic election. The election was won by the African National Congress (ANC) with Nelson Mandela as president.

### ▼ THE MODERN ECONOMY ▼

After the downfall of the Zulu Kingdom in 1879, many Zulu were absorbed into the South African economy as laborers. They became miners in parts of the former Transvaal, now renamed Gauteng, which means the Place of Gold. Today, many Zulu men still earn their livings as migrant workers in the mines and other urban centers. For much of the year, miners live in single-sex hostels. They only return to their rural homes and families for brief holidays.

However, the majority of urban blacks still live in townships, the residential areas for blacks, which were once located on the edges of South Africa's segregated cities. These urban dwellers work in the wide variety of occupations that make up any modern city in the world—ranging from factory and office workers, to doctors and lawyers.

Extensive changes were brought about by colonization, the system of migrant workers, and urbanization (the movement of people to the cities). However, many Zulu people maintain a

Today many Zulu people maintain strong ties to rural traditions. The traditional houses and skin clothing worn by the shepherd above are rarely seen today.

strong attachment to the land, cattle, and other aspects of Zulu tradition. Many who live and work in the cities still support a rural homestead with their earnings and regard the rural areas as their true home.

One of the problems facing the new, democratic government in South Africa is the redistribution of land that was taken from blacks throughout the course of history. This

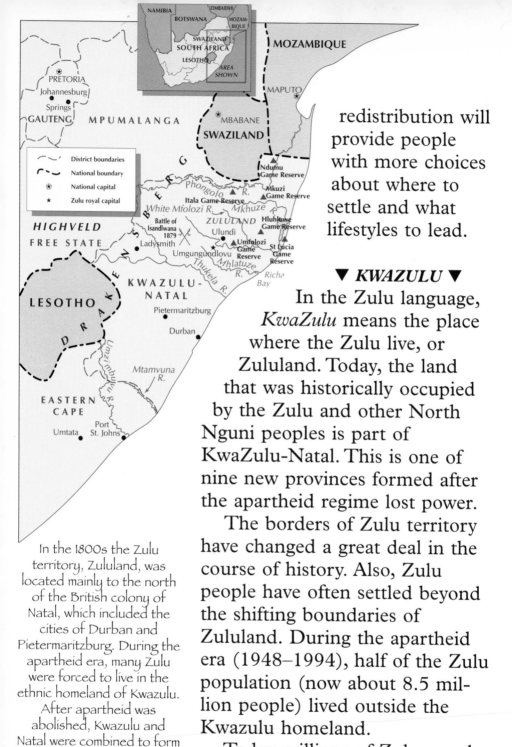

redistribution will provide people with more choices about where to settle and what lifestyles to lead.

## ▼ KWAZULU ▼

In the Zulu language, *KwaZulu* means the place where the Zulu live, or Zululand. Today, the land that was historically occupied by the Zulu and other North Nguni peoples is part of KwaZulu-Natal. This is one of nine new provinces formed after the apartheid regime lost power.

The borders of Zulu territory have changed a great deal in the course of history. Also, Zulu people have often settled beyond the shifting boundaries of Zululand. During the apartheid era (1948–1994), half of the Zulu population (now about 8.5 million people) lived outside the Kwazulu homeland.

Today millions of Zulu people live in the big cities and towns of

In the 1800s the Zulu territory, Zululand, was located mainly to the north of the British colony of Natal, which included the cities of Durban and Pietermaritzburg. During the apartheid era, many Zulu were forced to live in the ethnic homeland of Kwazulu. After apartheid was abolished, Kwazulu and Natal were combined to form the province of KwaZulu-Natal.

KwaZulu-Natal and other provinces of South Africa, particularly Durban and Johannesburg.

## ▼ POLITICAL TENSIONS ▼

From 1971 to 1994, Mangosuthu Buthelezi was the leader of the Kwazulu homeland. According to Zulu tradition, Buthelezi, as King Goodwill Zwelithini's uncle, should serve as the king's chief minister. In this case, however, King Zwelithini lacked any real political power in the homeland system. His powers had been greatly reduced after the destruction of the Zulu Kingdom. This has often led to tension between the king and Buthelezi.

The white-controlled South African government pressured the black-inhabited homelands to become first self-governing and then independent. Once the homelands declared their independence, the people lost their right to have South African citizenship. Unlike other homeland leaders, Buthelezi refused to accept independence. He continually worked to increase his power as the official representative of the Zulu people.

Since the 1980s, the KwaZulu-Natal region has experienced a lot of violence. This is partly because the ANC and the Inkatha Freedom Party, headed by Buthelezi, are both competing for the support of the Zulu people. These political parties have different visions of post-

Since the time of Shaka, the Zulu king has played a key role in Zulu affairs. Seen above is the current king, King Zwelethini, addressing guests at the wedding of a Zulu princess.

apartheid South Africa. Inkatha is an ethnic organization that strives to promote the culture and interests of the Zulu people. The ANC, on the other hand, aims to build a nation that unites people of all races and ethnic backgrounds.

To complicate matters, Inkatha is challenging the traditional role of the king in Zulu culture. Zulu nationalism and cultural identity have been centered around the king since Shaka's time. Today, Inkatha, a political party, would like to make itself the main channel through which Zulu culture is expressed.

This dispute has made culture more and more political. King Zwelethini wants to be the leader of all Zulu people, regardless of which political party they support. But Inkatha is not happy with the king's neutral role. The Inkatha Freedom Party insists that all Zulu people identify solely with its political goals. This has heightened tensions between King Zwelethini and Buthelezi.

## ▼ THE LAND ▼

KwaZulu-Natal receives the best rains in southern Africa. The climate is subtropical. It is hot and bushy along the coast; temperate and grassy towards the interior. It is ideal both for raising animals and farming. Rich wildlife that once filled the area is now found in game reserves.

By the end of the 1700s, this attractive area was densely populated. Profitable trade routes linked North Nguni chiefdoms with Portuguese and other European traders at Delagoa Bay (called Maputo today; the capital of Mozambique). Ivory was the key trade item. Powerful North Nguni chiefdoms began to compete for greater control over grazing land, trade routes, and other resources. The stage was set for Shaka's extraordinary rise to power.▲

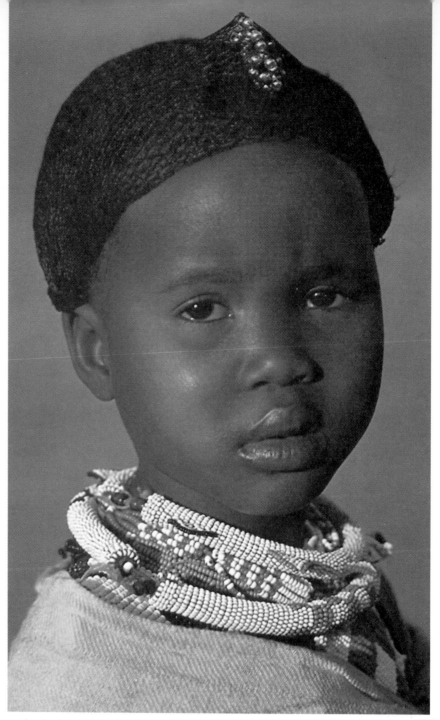

Cattle are the building block of traditional society. To marry, a man must pay his bride's family a number of cattle. This payment, called *lobola*, renders the couple's children legitimate. For this reason, a Zulu child such as this girl can be said to have been born "through the cow."

# chapter

# 2

# SOCIETY

**BEFORE SHAKA, THE ZULU AND NEIGHBORING** North Nguni groups had similar societies based on cattle herding.

### ▼ THE HOMESTEAD AND CATTLE ▼

The smallest unit of Zulu society was the homestead. A homestead, or family, consisted of a man, his wife or wives, their dependent children, and other relatives.

Each homestead was made up of a number of houses surrounding a cattle kraal, or corral. Cattle, herded by the men, were the physical and symbolic center of the homestead. They were also the basis of the family, since a man's family had to pay cattle to his bride's family in order to marry. This payment, called *lobola*, recognized the bride's family's contribution in raising her. It also compensated them for losing a member of their family.

The payment of *lobola* made a marriage legal. It was the basis of a man's rights over the children born during the marriage. A young man whose father had no cattle had very little chance of getting a wife and thus starting a new family.

Cattle were the measure of wealth and the key to political power. Because cattle could increase their number on their own, they were regarded as a form of investment. A wealthy man could lend some of his cows to a poorer neighbor or relation, who could live off their milk in exchange for tending the cows. In this way, a rich man could increase his power and influence in the community.

Cattle supplied milk and meat, as well as hides for clothing. They played a key role in meeting the physical needs of the people. They also played a vital role in spiritual life, which centered on the worship of the ancestors.

According to Zulu belief, the spirits of dead family members visit the living from time to time. The ancestors protect them from harm and bring them luck. The head of the household took charge of all religious ceremonies that communicated with the ancestors. A cow was sacrificed to honor the ancestors' spirits during major ceremonies, such as weddings and funerals, and for other religious occasions.

The father of the homestead represented his family to the chief or king. In front of the kraal

## AMADLOZI (ANCESTORS)

When a person dies, their spirit wanders about for a while, waiting to become an ancestor. Shortly after the funeral, the family performs a ceremony called *ukubuyisa*, which means to bring back. During the ceremony, the spirit of the dead person is called back to the homestead as an ancestor. If *ukubuyisa* is not performed, the spirit of the dead person becomes restless and turns into a ghost that haunts people.

After *ukubuyisa*, *amadlozi*, the ancestors, participate in the everyday life of the household and influence each person's life. In the view of many Zulu people, an individual does not achieve success alone, but with the help of the ancestors. Ancestors are the protectors of their living relatives; they look out for them and sometimes warn them of coming dangers through dreams.

Ancestors are often addressed in both stressful and joyful times. They must be honored and given regular offerings as a sign of respect and gratitude. If this is not done, the ancestors may become upset. To punish their neglectful relatives, the ancestors can hinder a person's progress in life or make the person sick.

gate, he visited with other men. Here he negotiated all the affairs of the household with the outside world.

Today people living in the rural areas may sell a cow to get money for their children's school fees or to pay a daughter's wedding expenses. Many Zulu still value cattle. Young rural men working in cities often convert their earnings

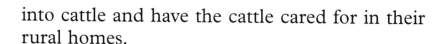

into cattle and have the cattle cared for in their rural homes.

### ▼ THE LAYOUT OF THE HOMESTEAD ▼

The houses of the homestead were arranged in a horseshoe-like formation around the kraal. There was one house for each wife, grown-up child, or relative. Each wife had a piece of land, her own household property, and a certain number of cattle. These were inherited by the oldest son of her house. The son could then choose to marry and establish his own homestead elsewhere.

Wives' houses were arranged in order of the wives' seniority. The *indlunkulu* (great house) at the far end of the homestead belonged to the "great wife." Not necessarily the first wife, she was the designated mother of the homestead heir. She was specially chosen by the head of the homestead. She was regarded with respect and often jealousy by the other wives in the homestead.

Men of status usually waited until they were quite old before marrying their great wives. This ensured that their heir would be too young to threaten his father's power or life. When a chief died, his heir was often too young to rule. A relative of the dead chief usually acted as governor, or regent, until the chief's rightful heir came of age.

The senior wife lived on the right hand side of the great house. She was the first to be

This painting from the 1800s shows the layout of a Zulu homestead occupied by a single family.

married. On her right was the house of the second wife. Subsequent wives were ranked in order of their seniority below these two houses. Below the houses of the wives and their children were the houses of the bachelors and other dependents. The homestead head lived in a house of his own and visited the houses of his wives every now and then.

Traditional Zulu houses were made of wattle sticks stuck into the ground and arched at the top. The structure was then covered with a thick layer of thatched grass artistically woven onto the wattle structure. The doorway was a small, low arch through which people crawled in and out. The floor of the house was made of clay and coated with dung. The dung was used to harden the clay. It also produced acids that

27

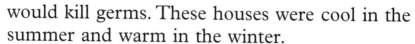

would kill germs. These houses were cool in the summer and warm in the winter.

Today, traditional houses and homestead layouts are rarely seen, since few men have more than one wife. Now most rural homesteads include some rectangular houses made of cement brick with corrugated iron roofs. Sometimes they also contain *rondavels*, round, thatched houses with earthen walls. Of course Zulu city dwellers today live in houses and apartments like everyone else in South Africa's big cities.

### ▼ WOMEN AND FARMING ▼

Cattle distinguished the rich from the poor. They also gave men economic and spiritual power over women. Although women were not allowed to handle the cattle, they did tend to the family's farm. The Zulu and their neighbors practiced a dual economy that combined herding with farming. Women's farming efforts fed the family.

The women planted small vegetable gardens close to the homesteads. A little farther away lay fields of staple crops such as sorghum, millet, and, later, corn. Women also planted pumpkins and collected wild vegetables.

Homestead women grew as much food as they needed for their families. Homesteads could distribute their produce however they saw fit. The chief and the king were also entitled to claim a certain portion.

Zulu women living in rural areas can often be recognized by their red headdresses. The designs of headdresses and beadwork vary according to region.

The woman on the right has stretched her ear lobes to fit colorful disks. Her apron, made

from a hide, shows that she is pregnant.

Since the introduction of the plow, men have become involved in tilling the soil. But weeding and harvesting are still largely left to women in the rural areas of KwaZulu-Natal.

## ▼ CHILDHOOD ▼

The education of children began at the homestead. Zulu boys learned to take care of herd animals at an early age. Girls were trained to farm and manage the daily chores of the household, such as fetching water and cooking.

Grandmothers played a key role in the early education of children by telling stories. These tales taught the history of the family and of the nation, recalled the deeds and adventures of national heroes, and taught important Zulu morals and concepts.

## ▼ CLANS ▼

A Zulu clan, or extended family group, consists of descendants who trace their origins to a common male ancestor, after whom the clan is usually named. Clan members recognize one male elder as their leader and religious head. Zulu clans may be widely scattered. Members of a clan did not, and still do not, marry within their own clan. Marriage is thus an important way of creating relationships between families as well as clans.

Members of a clan call each other father,

Marriage is one way of creating ties between Zulu clans. These women are married to a senior member of the Cele clan.

mother, sister, or brother, depending on how their families are related. For example, in a Zulu home, children treat their father with extreme respect and even awe, but they are more relaxed and open with their mother. They treat their father's siblings with great respect and formality, but are closer and more relaxed with their mother's siblings. The clan is thus held together by ties that are similar to those holding individual homes together.

This system of relations is still the basis of Zulu society today.

## ▼ CHIEFDOMS ▼

A group of clans occupying the same territory forms a chiefdom. The job of chief is hereditary;

Zulu chiefs are assisted by councillors called *izinduna*. Seen here is a group of senior officials at a public occasion.

that is, it is passed down from generation to generation in a certain family. The chiefdom took the name of the clan to which the chief belonged. For example, the Ngwane chiefdom was made up of a group of clans in which the Ngwane clan produced the chief for the whole group.

Unlike the clan, which is based on family ties, the chiefdom is a political organization in which people have customary rights and duties that are regulated by the laws of the chiefdom. In the past the chief was the custodian of the law.

The chiefs, in turn, had their own helpers, called *izinduna* (singular: *induna*) or heads. People took disputes first to an *induna*. If he

32

could not settle it, it would be referred to the chief, and, if necessary, to the king. The chief could appoint clan heads as councillors who advised him in trying and judging cases.

## ▼ THE KING ▼

Shaka united all the clans under his authority and became the first king. He controlled the army, and could replace chiefs at will. The king had a council of advisors, whose opinion he could take into consideration when making decisions.

The king's subjects were obliged to plant and harvest his fields. They also fought for him and surrendered to him all goods taken from the enemy during wartime. The king distributed some of his surplus, particularly captured cattle. He was the religious leader, and his ancestors were supposed to protect the whole nation against enemies. He was the highest judge in the land. The king held the sole power to pass the death penalty.

The numerous neighboring groups that Shaka defeated were all absorbed into the Zulu Kingdom. They had to pledge allegiance to the king and adopt the Zulu language and customs. Although the Zulu Kingdom was destroyed in 1879, the hereditary title of the Zulu king continues today. The present-day king is King Goodwill Zwelethini.

## CARVING

Before this century, Zulu wood sculptors, who were exclusively men, rarely carved human figures. Instead they produced beautiful, simple shapes and designs. These often reflect the religious and cultural importance of cattle in very subtle ways. For example, wooden Zulu milk pails, meat plates, spoons, and headrests often include areas of raised bumps. These are known as the *amasumpa* pattern and represent a herd of cattle, as if seen from above. Because cattle are so closely associated with the ancestors, using everyday objects with this pattern has a spiritual meaning. Objects made of cattle horn, such as snuff containers, have similar religious connections.

Experts believe that this unusual headrest was carved by a Zulu or North Nguni carver in the 1800s. Most Zulu headrests have simple shapes and patterns that suggest cattle. But this example is very clearly an image of a powerful bull. The belly has been hollowed out to serve as a container.

### ▼ HUNTING AND TRADE ▼

In earlier times the men were responsible for hunting. Associated with bravery, hunting was more often done for the adventure and the challenge rather than for the food.

Products obtained from the hunt were important luxury items. Sometimes, men were sent to hunt a lion or leopard to make clothing from the skin for their chief or king. The person whose spear killed the animal would gain great honor.

Elephant ivory was also a prestigious item. As the owner of the land, the chief was entitled to the one tusk that lay on the earth whenever an elephant was killed within the boundaries of his chiefdom. Many other products, such as fancy feathers, were similarly given to chiefs as tribute, or a sign of respect, by those under their authority.

Many trade routes linked the peoples of southern Africa before the arrival of the whites. Prestige items worn by people of high status (such as ivory and feathers) and metals for tools and weapons were particularly important. Trade with whites began in earnest through Delagoa Bay. Between 1750 and 1830 Africans traded here with the Portuguese, Dutch, and English. Chiefdoms in the region competed for control of the trade in ivory and other items. They became increasingly warlike. It was against this backdrop that Shaka rose to dominate the peoples and the economy of the entire region.▲

chapter

# 3
# SHAKA

**UNTIL SHAKA, THE ZULU CHIEFDOM WAS**
small. It consisted of about 2,000 people living
in a small area between the Mhlathuzi and
White Mfolozi rivers. In the late 1700s
Senzangakhona was the Zulu chief. He had an
affair with Nande, a woman from a neighboring
group. Senzangakhona's people could not believe
that Nande was pregnant with his child. They
said Nande was only suffering from *itshaka,* an
insect that causes stomach swelling. After Nande
gave birth, Senzangakhona married her. Her son
was named after the bug: Shaka.

### ▼ SHAKA'S UNHAPPY CHILDHOOD ▼
Senzangakhona, ashamed of his actions,
treated Nande and Shaka harshly. He finally
made them leave the royal homestead when
Shaka was six. Nande took her son back to her

36

own family. In Zulu culture, a marriage break-
down was usually seen as the wife's fault, for
failing to respect and obey her husband. Nande
is said to have been very stubborn and strong
willed. Following customs, Nande's parents
returned her *lobola* to her ex-husband. They
were ashamed of her, and treated her and Shaka
badly. Shaka came to resent his other relatives
and had a very lonely childhood. However, he
always remained close to his mother, Nande.

When Shaka was fifteen his mother, fearing
that Senzangakhona might try to kill him, sent
him away to her relatives among the Qwabe
people. Shaka also had a bad time there, so he
was sent to Nande's father's sister among the
Mthethwa people. Here Shaka grew to manhood.
Still today, a Zulu will often greet a Mthethwa
person with the praise, *Wena owakhulisa inkosi*,
meaning, "You who raised the king."

### ▼ LEARNING FROM DINGISWAYO ▼

In 1808 Dingiswayo became chief of the
Mthethwa. Dingiswayo grew in power by in-
creasing the strength of his army.

In the past young men of the North Nguni
peoples were initiated into adulthood. This initi-
ation lasted over several weeks or months and
took place in a secluded area. At the end of the
ceremony, the young men were circumcised.
After this they became adult men, free to marry,

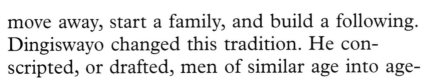

move away, start a family, and build a following. Dingiswayo changed this tradition. He conscripted, or drafted, men of similar age into age-regiments, called *amabutho* (singular: *butho*).

*Butho* members were summoned from their various homes to fight against rival chiefdoms. Men from conquered groups were merged into the victor's regiments, enlarging the army. As Dingiswayo's chiefdom grew, other weaker groups, such as the Zulu, voluntarily became his vassals, or loyal subjects. For paying an annual tribute, or tax, and fighting loyally for the Mthethwa chief, the vassals were offered protection, yet retained their independence.

With these changes, the Mthethwa chiefdom grew. It also became more centralized, because adult men could no longer break away from the main group to start their own followings. Similar changes occurred in other competing North Nguni chiefdoms, including the Ndwandwe, Ngwane, Qwabe, and Hlubi.

Dingiswayo expanded his chiefdom through warfare and diplomacy. One of his goals as a leader was to increase trade and control the port at Delagoa Bay, which he had visited as a young man. Shaka paid close attention to Dingiswayo's leadership skills and became a distinguished warrior in his army.

In 1816, when Shaka was twenty-nine years old, the Zulu chief, Senzangakhona, died.

Dingiswayo loaned some soldiers to Shaka to seize the chiefdom from Sigujana, one of Senzangakhona's sons. Shaka used and improved upon many of Dingiswayo's military practices. In this way, Shaka turned the small Zulu chiefdom into a highly effective fighting force.

In 1818 Dingiswayo was captured and killed by his main rival, Zwide of the Ndwandwe people. Shaka took control of the Mthethwa chiefdom. With the joint forces of the Zulu and Mthethwa under his control, Shaka began to build his empire.

### ▼ MILITARY METHODS ▼

Shaka's great military innovation was to make the army permanent. Instead of permitting *butho* members to live at home, he made them live in military barracks. Each regiment was led by a general, and based at one of Shaka's or *induna*'s (plural: *izinduna*), many royal homesteads.

Each royal homestead was the home of many of Shaka's concubines. Shaka feared heirs and never married; all women pregnant by him were executed. In the absence of the king, the favorite and most senior concubine of the household and the *induna* were responsible for the settlement.

Young women were also organized into non-fighting regiments. When Shaka disbanded a men's regiment, he also disbanded a female one from which he selected wives for his men. Prior to this no warrior could marry.

Shaka's soldiers were highly motivated. While in their regiments, Zulu men were not allowed to marry. They could only become men after they had proven their bravery and loyalty to the king. The regiments and individuals competed for the glory of the king's approval. Each regiment had its own name, distinctive color shield, and a war costume that might include prestigious decorations, such as rare feathers or skins. Shaka supplied these outfits

This is a rare picture of Sha It is based on a sketch tha was made by an English trac who knew Shaka. Here the Zulu king holds a long shie and a broad-bladed spear These weapons gave his arm a great advantage over their opponents.

to and provided for all the other daily needs of his soldiers.

Zulu soldiers underwent constant drills to perfect the new warfare techniques they learned. Shaka insisted on the use of short, broad-bladed stabbing spears. After their enemies threw their long spears, Shaka's warriors moved in with these deadly weapons. To protect against airborne spears, Zulu warriors carried large tough shields that covered most of their bodies.

The Zulu army advanced in a crescent-shaped battle formation called "cows' horns." This consisted of a "chest" of several regiments, together with one regiment on either side that formed a "horn." The horns served as pincers, or flanks, that closed in on the enemy from the sides, while the chest, in the middle, bore the brunt of the fighting.

Shaka made his soldiers train and fight without sandals, so that they could run faster than their enemies who tried to flee—any Zulu soldier who fled a battle was executed. Shaka also used guerrilla tactics and psychological weapons. His warriors tried to intimidate their enemies by beating their shields or yelling war cries. Their discipline and motivation made Shaka's soldiers practically invincible.

By 1826, when Shaka finally crushed Zwide of the Ndwandwe people, he controlled most of the territory formerly occupied by various North Nguni chiefdoms.

## COSTUME

Costume making was a highly developed Zulu art form. A person's clothes reflected his or her identity.

The clothing of every regiment and officer of the Zulu army could be immediately recognized. When dressed for ceremonial occasions, the king, chiefs, and other leading figures were distinguished by prestigious aspects of their costume, particularly leopard skin, ivory, and glass beads. In the past the distribution of such items was closely controlled by the king. Today these animal products are rare because wild animals are protected. Beads, however, are easier to obtain, because they are now less expensive than they were in the 1800s.

Each regiment in the army had its own uniform, or war dress. The costly hides and decorations were supplied by the king.

## DANCE

Shaka's warriors performed war dances in which they sang songs of bravery and daring. To create the rhythm, the men stamped their feet as they beat their shields or clapped their hands. This was often accompanied by beating drums. The combined effect of the drumming, singing, and highly energetic and aggressive dance steps was often enough to make an enemy flee in terror.

Sacred dances were performed at special ceremonies such as first fruit festivals. Today Zulu dances are performed in places as different as Shembe Church gatherings, at the mines, and at political rallies all over the country.

## ▼ THE FORMATION OF THE ▼ ZULU KINGDOM

The Zulu Kingdom grew in size and strength as Shaka brought the defeated tribes under his control. Shaka spared those groups who acknowledged his authority and became his vassals. They were forced to adopt the Zulu language, customs, and traditions. The young men were drafted into the Zulu army, and often many of their women and cattle were taken. Defeated people sometimes remained under their own chiefs, who then directly answered to Shaka.

Shaka often appointed his own relatives as chiefs in distant areas. This ensured loyalty in remote regions. Equally important, this kept the king's rivals out of the way. There is a saying among the Zulu that a king will not eat out of the same bowl as his brothers for fear that they might poison him.

Apart from being the supreme commander and absolute ruler, Shaka also became the religious head of the kingdom. Since rain was crucial to their lives for grazing and farming, North Nguni peoples had traditional rainmakers in their societies. Rainmakers were highly regarded as people who had the spiritual power to bring rain. Shaka banished or killed all rainmakers in his kingdom and assumed this role himself.

The Zulu also believed that the success of their crops was due to the blessings of their ancestors. They developed a thanksgiving ceremony at the beginning of each harvest to honor the ancestors and pray for the following year's harvest. Shaka abolished the performance of this First Fruits ceremony by chiefs. He turned it into a public display of his military might, with himself as its central focus. This festival is no longer celebrated today.

By assuming these spiritual roles, Shaka became a symbolic giver of life and sustainer of his people. For this his people respected him and felt that they owed him their lives.

## ▼ SHAKA'S DEATH ▼

Shaka's military exploits gave the Zulu a great sense of pride in their nation. But Shaka

## MFECANE

"Mfecane," which means the great scattering in Nguni languages, was the result of the changes that occurred in Shaka's time. The entire southern African region was destabilized. Many chiefdoms were scattered by warfare or fled in all directions from the growing power of Shaka and other rival chiefdoms. Some of Shaka's generals and vassal chiefs deserted and moved away. They hoped to build up their own states beyond Shaka's reach.

Some North Nguni groups fled west over the Drakensberg Mountains onto the Highveld plateau. There they disrupted the Sotho-Tswana peoples.

In the 1820s a devastating drought made food scarce in the region. Several fleeing communities rapidly became starving raiders. They were desperate and attacked other settled people to get food. Any group that was overrun had no choice but to join the raiders or starve. Soon this process snowballed. Thousands died or were killed. Some people became cannibals in order to survive.

Most powerful among the groups that moved onto the Highveld were the Khumalo under Mzilikazi, one of Shaka's best generals. Other groups who fled across the Drakensberg were the Hlubi under Mpangazitha, and the Ngwane under Matiwane.

Other refugees fled south and settled among the Xhosa-speaking South Nguni people. They called the newcomers Mfengu, meaning beggars. Another famous general, Shoshangane, settled with his people in southern Mozambique and formed a kingdom called Gaza, after Soshangane's father. Other groups, known today as the Ngoni, battled their way as far north as Malawi and Tanzania.

The Mfecane thus produced great changes throughout southern Africa and far beyond. The Zulu Kingdom grew to power during this period. So did another kingdom, composed largely of refugees from the Mfecane: the Basotho of King Moshoeshoe. However, the Mfecane caused so much havoc and suffering that most surviving groups were left weak and vulnerable at a crucial moment: just when whites, hungry for land, began to move into the interior of South Africa.

became a military dictator. He ruled with an iron fist, killing all his opponents. He punished his soldiers severely for losing battles and put to death all soldiers who lost their assegais, or spears, in war. It is said that vultures perpetually circled around the place where Shaka had people executed, waiting for fresh bodies.

When his beloved mother Nande died in 1827, Shaka killed about 7,000 people. He wanted other families to share his grief by losing their own loved ones. Many were killed for not crying enough. In addition Shaka imposed a mourning period of one year during which no farming was permitted. This meant hunger for his people.

Toward the end of his rule, Shaka was more feared than respected by both his people and his army leaders. In 1828 Shaka was running short of people to raid in order to feed his expanding army. He sent his army south of the Mzimvubu River to raid the Pondo. But before his returning soldiers had even rested, Shaka sent them north to raid the Soshangane. Shaka's half brothers, Dingane and Mhlangane, sneaked away from the war-weary army to assassinate Shaka. When the army returned from the campaign, Dingane was on the throne. Expecting a heavy punishment from Shaka for losing the battle against Soshangane, the army must have been relieved to find Shaka dead. This alone was probably reason enough for them to accept Dingane. ▲

## CHRISTIANITY

By about 1835, Christian missionaries began to enter Zululand. By condemning Zulu traditions and customs, they hoped to have the Zulu convert to Christianity.

Today, the majority of people belong to one of many Christian groups. Of particular importance are African Independent Churches. They combine many Zulu beliefs and customs into Christian worship. Worship of the ancestors is the foundation for some of these churches. They argue that the ancestors in African culture play the same role as the saints in Western culture. Healing with spiritual power is a key aspect of these churches. Some spiritual healers use holy water while others practice laying on of hands.

The Shembe Church, founded in 1910, blends Zulu traditions with Christian worship. Worshippers' costumes indicate their status. The dancers seen above belong to a church regiment for married women.

# 4

## AFTER SHAKA

**WHITE FOREIGNERS BEGAN TO ENCROACH**
upon the land of the Zulu in the early 1800s.
Most of this land was later lost to the whites.
The Zulu suffered major losses of land as a
result of the founding of Port Natal (the city of
Durban today) by the British and the Natalia
Republic by the Boers.

### ▼ PORT NATAL ▼

Natal, which means birth in Portuguese, had
first been named by the Portuguese explorer
Vasco da Gama when he sailed by on Christmas
Day in 1497. In 1824 Shaka allowed a small
group of whites from the Cape Colony to establish a settlement at Port Natal. Shaka and the
newcomers were eager to trade with each other.
Shaka was impressed and curious about the new
items that the whites showed him, including

muskets and medicines. He is said to have given the whites a piece of land around Port Natal that spread thirty-five miles along the coast and 100 miles inland.

According to Zulu custom, the land, like the people themselves, belonged to the king. He loaned farms to people under his authority; no one actually owned the land they had been granted. Shaka never imagined, therefore, that when he loaned land to the whites, they believed themselves to be the owners. Shaka regarded Port Natal as part of his kingdom and its local leaders as his subjects.

Shaka had unknowingly provided whites with the foothold they would later use to destroy his kingdom and gain control of the land.

### ▼ DINGANE'S RULE (1828–1838) ▼

Dingane tried to hold together the empire that Shaka had established. But many allies broke away under his rule. By the 1830s many Zulu had settled south of the Thukela River among the whites of Port Natal. Because they took in Zulu refugees, Dingane realized that the whites did not regard themselves as his subjects.

Like Shaka before him, Dingane began to impose his authority through very harsh methods. For example, in 1831 Captain Allen Gardiner of Port Natal agreed to return to Dingane any Zulu subjects who fled to Port

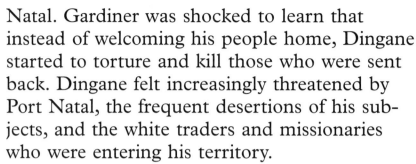

Natal. Gardiner was shocked to learn that instead of welcoming his people home, Dingane started to torture and kill those who were sent back. Dingane felt increasingly threatened by Port Natal, the frequent desertions of his subjects, and the white traders and missionaries who were entering his territory.

Tension increased with the arrival of the Boers, which means farmers in the Dutch language. The Boers moved away from areas that were under British control. They hoped to set up their own independent republics free of the British.

The Boers, cattle herders like the Zulu, began to settle throughout Zulu territory without permission from the Zulu king. It was clear that the land the Zulu had fought so hard to gain was under threat.

In February 1838, a party of Boers led by Piet Retief, visited Dingane's kraal to finalize a land grant. The Boers had been promised land if they returned some Zulu cattle that had been stolen by the Tlokwa chief Sekonyela. To carry out this mission, Retief had visited Sekonyela and tricked him into trying on a pair of handcuffs, which he then locked. The humiliated chief agreed to return the cattle.

Some of the Zulu observers who had gone with Retief thought that his powers seemed unreal and suspected him of witchcraft. Dingane had underestimated the power of the Boers. He believed that the Boers would be wiped out by the Tlokwa, but his hopes were in vain. In fact the Boers had also defeated Mzilikazi, Shaka's former general who led the strongest African force on the Highveld. The Boers' muskets gave them a tremendous advantage over Zulu warriors armed only with spears.

Retief and his party of Boers returned to Dingane to pressure him to give them the land he had promised. Dingane signed the treaty and invited them to a dance of celebration the following day. In the middle of the celebration, he let out the cry, "Seize the wizards," and his warriors dragged the Boers off to their execution.

This picture of King Dingane was drawn by Captain Allen Gardiner. He was a missionary who settled in Natal in 1835, and knew the king. Other drawings by Gardiner appear on the following two pages.

These drawings show King Dingane dressed for a grand dance held at the capital of the Zulu Kingdom. His costumes consist of beadwork, feathers, and fur. Beads were rare and expensive at this time. The king's armbands are made of ivory and metal. All these precious materials indicate the king's rank and wealth. Dingane is said to have liked these pictures. He thought they were very realistic.

As Dingane had planned, Boer settlements throughout Zulu territory were attacked over the next few months. About 300 Boers and 200 of their attendants were killed, and many cattle stolen. The Boers were in a very dangerous position. So were the English at Port Natal, who attacked Dingane. The British also suffered a devasting attack and took refuge on a ship in the harbor of Port Natal.

In an effort to avenge their murdered

52

These pictures were drawn at the same occasion as the pictures on page 52. The woman on the left is one of the king's dancers. The woman on the right seems to be bowing before the king. Nobody was ever allowed to stand higher than the king. If he was seated, others had to crawl in his presence.

comrades the Boers organized a commando, or group of raiders, consisting of 470 men under Andries Pretorius. They pulled their wagons into a defensive circle, called a *laager*, in the hope of withstanding the full might of the Zulu army. Before the battle, they prayed to God for help. They vowed to treat the anniversary of the battle as holy if they won. Inside the *laager*, from between and beneath the wagons, they fired their guns and cannons at the Zulu, who had no firearms. The battle was fought on the banks of the Ncome River on December 16, 1838. Over 3,000 Zulu warriors died in the battle. It is said that their blood turned the waters of the Ncome red. To this day the event is known as the Battle of Blood River.

Until 1990, December 16 was commemorated by Afrikaners (descendants of the Boers) as a public holiday called the Day of the Vow. Because they thought their miraculous victory was a sign that they were God's chosen people, they believed themselves to be superior to black people. This was considered a racially charged holiday, because Afrikaners and some other whites celebrated a victory that the Zulu and other blacks saw as a slaughter. This holiday has now been changed to the Day of Reconciliation.

### ▼ NATALIA AND NATAL ▼

After their victory, the Boers found the legal document Dingane had signed, giving them rights to the territory which they called the Natalia Republic. They established their capital at Pietermaritsburg. They took over all Zulu territory south of the Thukela River.

Dingane was forced to pay a huge sum in cattle and turn over the land between the Thukela River and St. Lucia Bay. Dingane ordered his people to withdraw from the Thukela and then relocate to the Umfolozi.

Morale among the remainder of Dingane's army was so low that his own half-brother, Mpande, deserted with a considerable number of followers. He formed an alliance with the Boers against Dingane. Mpande's army met Dingane's at the Battle of Magongo in 1840.

In heavy fighting, many of the remaining Zulu warriors died. Mpande was victorious; Dingane fled to Swaziland where he was assassinated by a minor Swazi chief. Mpande was declared king by the Boers on the condition that he remain at peace with them. Mpande paid over 50,000 cattle as tribute to the Boers. The power of the mighty Zulu Kingdom had been smashed.

With the decline of the kingdom's power, thousands of people who had fled Zululand began to return to their original homes. But most of the territory had already been taken over by Boers. The situation quickly became unstable.

The British became alarmed when the government of Natalia planned to expel these refugees to the south as this would threaten the British position. A British army was sent to reinforce Port Natal. There, the British were besieged by the Boers. However, the Boers knew they needed help to hold the Zulu territory they had taken. After much debate, the Boers agreed to let the British control the coast, while they ran the interior. Within a few years, Boer unity broke down while British control strengthened. In 1845 Britain made Natal part of the Cape Colony.

### ▼ THE END OF THE KINGDOM ▼

Under Mpande's long and peaceful rule (1840–1872), the Zulu population and its herds regained strength. Meanwhile, thousands of British settlers began to settle Natal.

Mpande was succeeded by his son, Cetshwayo, who attempted to remain on good terms with the British. This irritated the British high commissioner, Sir Bartle Frere, who believed that the Zulu Kingdom had to be destroyed.

Despite strict instructions from the officials in London not to provoke the Zulus, Frere was determined to go to war. When a minor Zulu chief chased after two unfaithful wives who crossed into Natal and captured them, Frere treated it as a major international incident. He gave Cetshwayo twenty days to hand over the kidnappers and pay a fine of cattle. Cetshwayo agreed to this. Frere also ordered Cetshwayo to disband the Zulu regimental system and allow a British diplomat to supervise. This would mean the surrender of the kingdom and the end of the Zulu social system. Cetshwayo could not do this.

When the ultimatum expired, British troops invaded Zululand. They could not know that the Zulu were about to win the greatest victory over

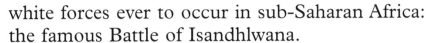

white forces ever to occur in sub-Saharan Africa: the famous Battle of Isandhlwana.

A large portion of the British army had camped on the side of a hill called Isandhlwana. Unknown to them, the Zulu army had approached undetected through the hilly country. With great courage, in the face of bullets against which they were defenseless, the Zulu army overran the entire British force. More than 1,400 British soldiers were killed. The military defeat at this battle disgraced the British Army and severely dented the prestige of the British Empire.

The war raged on for months, with heavy losses on the Zulu side. Finally, the British attacked Cetshwayo's capital at Ulundi on July 4, 1879, and defeated what was left of the Zulu army. About 2,000 Zulu were killed by rifle and machine gun fire. The capital of Ulundi was burned; Cetshwayo was imprisoned in Cape Town. This was the end of the independent Zulu Kingdom.

### ▼ COLONIAL RULE AFTER 1879 ▼

The British divided up the Zulu Kingdom into thirteen chiefdoms. They restored the independence of chiefdoms like the Mthethwa and Ndwandwe that had been brought under Shaka's control. Members of the Zulu royal family were humiliated by being placed under the control of British favorites who had no connection to Shaka's line.

The resulting tensions, which have caused many lasting problems, led to the outbreak of the Zulu civil war in 1881. In 1883 Cetshwayo was returned to Zululand as chief of a small part of his previous kingdom. The civil war continued. After he was defeated, Cetshwayo took refuge with the British in 1884. He died under suspicious circumstances, and many Zulu believed he was murdered.

Cetshwayo's son, Dinizulu, succeeded him and led the royalist faction. The Boers helped Dinizulu defeat his enemies. In return, they demanded 3 million acres of prime grazing land. They also attempted to make Zululand their protectorate, a territory under Boer control.

Fearing the loss of his kingdom, Dinizulu appealed to the British instead. They responded by both making Zululand a British protectorate in 1887 *and* giving the Boers the land they wanted. Dinizulu had lost both land and control. Following clashes with the British, Dinizulu was exiled to St. Helena, a tiny island in the Atlantic Ocean.

In 1897 Zululand finally became part of the British colony of Natal. Dinizulu was brought back from exile, but given very little power. As in other crushed African states under British control, Zulu chiefs became, in effect, employees of the British Empire. They were forced to

## PRAISE POETRY

During Shaka's time, the king had his own praise poet who composed and recited the king's praises during public gatherings. The praises often referred to historical events, so they were an important way of remembering history. Today, oral history is being written down to preserve the important knowledge it contains.

Contemporary praise poetry has now also become a form of popular music. Mzwakhe Mbuli, also known as The People's Poet, draws on Zulu traditional praise forms to deal with current issues. He performed at the presidential inauguration of Nelson Mandela.

Praise poets continue to compose praises to South African leaders. Seen here are President Nelson Mandela (left) and Mangosuthu Buthelezi, who is the current political leader of KwaZulu-Natal.

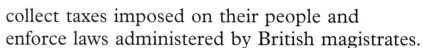

collect taxes imposed on their people and enforce laws administered by British magistrates.

Much of Zululand was sold to whites, but Zulu people were taxed to pay for its administration. Conditions in Zululand were desperate. These factors provoked a Zulu rebellion in 1906, led by a minor chief called Bambatha. In the Bambatha Rebellion, British colonial forces killed between 3,000 and 4,000 Zulus and arrested 7,000. Dinizulu, suspected of playing a role in the rebellion, was arrested in 1907. In 1910, while he was in prison, the Boer republics and the British colonies of the Cape and Natal finally united to form the modern country of South Africa.

What little land remained in black hands was systematically taken away by legislation, beginning with the infamous 1913 Native Land Act. Black people were confined to infertile reserves where they suffered from malnutrition and diseases.

From that time onward, although the South African government tolerated and recognized the Zulu royal line of succession, the Zulu king was no longer the political leader of his people.

Today the Zulu people play key roles both in KwaZulu-Natal and in South Africa as a whole. Many of them maintain a strong sense of pride in their history and their traditions.▲

# Glossary

**Afrikaner** A person of Dutch descent who settled in southern Africa.

*amasumpa* A pattern of raised bumps, representing cattle, that is used as a decoration.

ANC (**African National Congress**) The leading political party in South Africa.

**apartheid** The South African system of racial and ethnic segregation.

**assegai** A slender spear.

*butho* (**plural:** *amabutho*) A regiment of people of similar age.

**diviner** A person who sees future events by interpreting omens.

**homelands** Ethnic reservations where black South Africans were forced to live.

*induna* (**plural:** *izinduna*) Advisors, or helpers, to Zulu chiefs and kings.

**kraal** Corral; a livestock pen.

**laying on of hands** A healer places his or her hands on a sick person in order to heal him or her.

*lobola* A payment, usually in the form of cattle, that a groom's family makes to his bride's.

**tribute** A payment, tax, or gift given to a ruler as the price of protection or to show respect.

# For Further Reading

Bryant, A. T. *Olden Times in Natal and Zululand.* London: Longmans, 1929.

———. *A History of the Zulu.* Cape Town: Struik, 1964.

Fuze, Magema. *Black People and Whence they Came: A Zulu View.* Durban: Natal University Press, 1979.

Hammond-Tooke, David. *The Roots of Black South Africa.* Johannesburg: Jonathan Ball, 1993.

Morris, Jean, and Eleanor Preston-White. *Speaking with Beads: Zulu Arts from Southern Africa.* New York: Thames and Hudson, 1994.

Mutwa, Vusamazulu Credo. *Indaba My Children.* Johannesburg: Blue Crane Books, 1964.

Omer-Cooper, John D. *History of Southern Africa.* 2nd ed. Portsmouth, NH: Heinemann, 1994.

*Challenging Reading*

Berglund, A. I. *Zulu Thought-Patterns and Symbolism.* Cape Town: David Philip, 1976.

Duminy, A. and B. Guest, eds. *Natal and Zululand from Earliest Times to 1910: A New History.* Pietermaritzburg: Natal University Press, 1989.

# Index

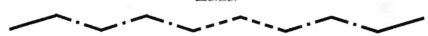

## About the Author
Born in Lamontville, KwaZulu-Natal, Zolani Ngwane has a background in both theology and anthropology, and a special interest in the theory of colonial space. He has earned two master's degrees, one from the Divinity School of the University of Chicago and the other from the Chicago Theological Seminary. A doctoral candidate in the Department of Anthropology at the University of Chicago, Mr. Ngwane is currently conducting research for his dissertation entitled *The Politics of Campus and Community in South Africa: An Historical Ethnography of the University of Fort Hare.*

## Photo Credits
Cover, pp. 8, 13, 15, 20, 29, 47 by Jean Morris © McGregor Museum; pp. 11, 17, 31, 32 by Aubrey Elliot © McGregor Museum; p. 27 © MuseuMAfrica; p. 34 Southern African Art Collection © The Brenthurst Library, Johannesburg; pp. 40, 42, 51, 52, 53 © South African Library; p. 59 © Southlight/Gamma Liaison.

## Consulting Editor
Gary N. van Wyk, Ph.D.

## Layout and Design
Kim Sonsky